CONTENTS

ACKNOWLEDGE-MENTS

There are many people who deserve thanks for helping me put this together.

First, I want to thank Mike Gelb, a dear friend, who even though in retirement, said he would take on one more writing project. I am grateful for his assistance not only because he is a gifted writer but because as a lay person when it comes to real estate, estates, and law, he was able to make sure we didn't go too far into the legal and technical weeds.

I also want to thank Scott Flanders, Doug Wade and Thomas Sadler who run Northern Virginia Title and Escrow, my "go to" settlement folks for over 2 decades. I know my cases aren't always the easiest, but I keep you on your toes. Thank you for reviewing the text and providing a few key comments and links.

Thanks also goes out to my brokers at RE/MAX Gateway, Scott MacDonald and David Werfel who also reviewed this book and provided additional insights. I joined RE/MAX Gateway in 2016 after the owner of my previous RE/MAX franchise decided to retire. I have enjoyed every minute of my time at Gateway. Great colleagues, great training, and great support all stemming from great leadership.

Another thank you goes to my assistant, Anna Kate Murphy. She has been instrumental in helping keep me on track and building the systems that have let me help so many families during a difficult time in their life. Anna Kate, I am so lucky to have been able to work with you these last few years.

Joe Facenda

But the most important thanks goes to my wife Mindy who stuck by me and supported me during those early lean (sometimes very lean) years. It would have been easy at times to abandon real estate and head back to the corporate world, but we plowed through and together were able to fully participate in raising our two wonderful boys, Jamie and Eli. Love you all.

FOREWORD

Chances are that you are holding this book because you have arrived at a critical and emotional point in your life. Most likely, one of your parents or some other family member has recently passed away or is approaching their final days, and you're thinking ahead. In addition to the human impact, you may be facing administrative and financial challenges that often come with death. One of the issues may be what to do about a house you've just inherited.

This book is designed to help by sharing the insights of a real estate professional who has helped scores of clients in this situation. Generally, you have three choices with the house – live in it, rent it, or sell it. This book will examine many of the issues you will have to consider and explains some of the things you will need to do.

WHO AM I TO THINK I CAN HELP?

I'm a Realtor® and proud of it. That's been my profession for 30 years, a career I began shortly after my oldest son was born. I'd been working for a major retail chain and was advancing in my career, but I had a boss I didn't like, and I wanted more control of my time so I could run to my son's school when needed, coach youth sports teams, and just be available for whatever came along. My wife and I had just bought our first house, and I was impressed by the way our Realtor helped us through the process. I had the bright idea that "I can do that." I loved the idea of working for myself, and I hoped I would get satisfaction from helping people like me become homeowners.

In the planning phase, becoming a Realtor sounded like a good idea, but then, I made $81 for the first six months. That was disappointing, to say the least. Fortunately, things got better quickly, and I've been at it ever since.

I've always done traditional transactions helping people buy and sell their personal homes. However, at different stages of my career, there have been different niches I worked at a little more than others. When I first started, it was first time homebuyers. I'd just been in the same boat, understood that mindset and believed that as their life changed – marriage, children, job promotions, relocations and the like – I would be positioned for their future business.

Then, during and after the financial crisis of 2008, investors became a healthy percentage of my business. I became a student of the investment mindset. Some were buy-and-hold investors. Some were "flippers," who renovated and resold distressed properties. I was particular about who I worked with because I wasn't comfortable with the business practices of some flippers.

Observing investors led me to another niche -- sales involving inherited properties. I saw families at their most vulnerable make poor decisions and sell to an investor when they could easily do better with a different strategy. Investors provide a needed service and play an important role in the housing market, but some of what I saw disturbed me. More on that later.

Additionally, in recent years, as I have aged and my own parents have aged, I have come to a deep understanding of the issues – sometimes complicated ones – facing a family at this emotional time. And as with my early years helping first-time buyers, I have found it personally gratifying to help folks through situations they found complicated and hard to navigate.

Over the years, I've won many awards and am consistently one of the top producers in our region. But you will never see me as the #1 agent in the market, and there is a specific reason for that. I believe each client needs personal attention. Personal attention takes time. I know that the time I devote to each buyer or seller is more than average. I will go above and beyond to do little things that are outside of official Realtor duties to make the process easier for my clients. This is particularly true for those selling an inherited property – especially those who have moved away from where their parents lived and are trying to do it long distance.

Please keep this in mind when selecting a Realtor for your transaction. There are many agents out there with great numbers, but if their business model is dependent upon doing more transactions than the next guy, it is possible they may not be able to give you the attention you need for this very important assignment.

On another note, I have been a long term volunteer and advocate for Habitat for Humanity and even spent two years as Chairman of my local affiliate. The Habitat Restores are a great resource for an heir who is prepping a house for sale. They are always my first choice for donating unwanted furniture and household goods.

TERMINOLOGY

Throughout this book, we may use certain terms that are not legally accurate at all times but illustrate the point.

For instance, we may use the word "heir" to mean the person inheriting the property. But legally, an heir is someone who gets the property when there is no will. If the property is inherited through a will, that person is a devisee. And if it comes through a trust, they may be called a beneficiary. For our purposes, heir means all of those - the person or people inheriting a property.

There are parts of the book where using the proper term is critical as some duties and responsibilities are different based on whether there was a will, no will or a trust. In those situations, we will use correct terms but, in general, I want to stay away from legalese or having to say "heir or devisee" when "heir" gets the message across.

There are also many different names for the person who is handling the estate. The words executor, administrator, curator, proponent of the will and, in the case of a trust, successor trustee, all refer to the person in charge. Throughout the book, we will be using the words executor and administrator interchangeably. The purpose of the book is to cover the big concepts. It is not a legal manual, so I want to keep it simple when possible. For goodness sake, technically a female executor is an executrix. That's way too much for me and not relevant to the issue at hand.

We will frequently talk about the home "mom and dad" left you because they are the ones most likely to leave you a house. But you may have inherited a house from another family member. Or, you may be the executor for a brother, sister, cousin, or other relative and will not receive any of the proceeds from the home sale. Whatever your specific situation, the guidelines in this book still apply.

The book discusses the possible sale of a house to an "investor." When I use that term, I am generally talking about someone who will buy the home, renovate it and sell it at a profit. It also can refer to a professional builder who may want to tear down the home you're selling and build a new house on the lot.

Last note… Whenever you see a book icon, it is story time. These stories actually happened. However, I have changed the names, locations, types of home and some other details for privacy reasons but the gist of the story is real and illustrates the issue at hand.

THIS IS NOT LEGAL ADVICE

Although the discussion in this book touches on some legal issues and the text has been reviewed by an attorney, this book focuses on real estate. It is not a substitute for an attorney in dealing with estate matters; nor does it tell you what to do about financial or tax issues you may face. Those matters are other people's specialties. I advise on how to buy and sell houses, townhouses, and condos.

PART 1: "WHERE DO I BEGIN?"

With your parent's passing, you now own (or are about to own) a house that wasn't yours the day before. Perhaps you've bought or sold a house before. Or, this might be the first time you've owned a piece of property, and you are unsure about this new responsibility. Maybe, inheriting a house will turn out to be a financial windfall, or you might find that you are digging out of a money mess that mom or dad unintentionally left behind. You may be the sole heir, or you may be a joint heir with other family members. No doubt, a family member's death is an emotional experience. The house itself may touch emotional chords especially if it's the one you grew up in. You may be uncertain where to start.

FIRST STEP: GETTING THE FACTS

You basically have three choices – live in the house, rent it, or sell it. Sometimes, but not too often, there's a fourth choice – walk away and let the bank (or mortgage company) take the house. But whatever the answer turns out to be – and it will differ with circumstances – you first need to assess the situation and after that, assess the house. Let's begin with the questions I would ask if you were my client:

Question 1 –Who are the decision-makers? Who needs to sign?

Ideally, there's a will (or a trust) because it removes uncertainty. A will spells out exactly who gets what, including real estate, and it eliminates the surprises that can happen when an unexpected or even unknown family member comes forward. Generally, a will designates one or two individuals to act as executor to dispose of the estate's assets and distribute them to the heirs as directed by the person who just passed away.

When it comes to real estate, the executor will be granted varying degrees of authority. He or she may be *directed* to sell the house or may be given the discretionary authority to sell the house, but not be ordered to do so. It's also possible, the power to sell the house is granted to the heirs with the executor helping to implement their decisions. More often than not, the executor is a family member who consults with other heirs about how to dispose of the house and any other real estate. Sometimes, the executor is not a family member, but more than likely he or she will work collaboratively with the heirs to decide what to do.

If the executor is directed to sell the home, that individual alone can sign all documents. If the executor is authorized, but not required, to sell the home, the title company may require other heirs to sign. Check with an attorney if your situation is unclear.

In some cases, a parent will leave a house to just one individual. That can create relationship issues if there are multiple siblings and some feel they've been slighted. But if that heir is also the executor, it simplifies the real estate transaction because there is only one decision-maker and that person is the only one who needs to sign related documents. Wills can be challenged in court when somebody feels wronged, but for the purposes of this discussion, we will assume that is not the situation in your case. If, however, the validity of the will becomes an issue, the sale process cannot proceed until a judge provides guidance to all involved.

If the deceased parent had more than one child or other relatives he or she was close to, the will might divide ownership of the house equally among them. That's usually what I've seen as a Realtor.

If your family member died without a will, the disposition of property is determined by state law. (For Virginia this link helps explain Intestate Succession https://law.lis.virginia.gov/vacode/title64.2/chapter2/section64.2-200/_)   In general, a spouse is first in line and children come next. If there is no living spouse, the state generally gives the assets to a couple's children in equal shares. But it there have been children from multiple relationships it can get much more complicated. Again, best to consult with an attorney if your situation is not clear cut.

In the absence of a will, decisions about the house *must* be shared among the heirs, and legal documents will require the signature of every heir. In this circumstance, a single heir can exercise effective veto power by refusing to sign documents relating to the house. Depending on the individuals involved, this can be a big hurdle or a little one. I've experienced both. Early in the process, the heirs will have to get together – either in person or by some electronic means – and make joint decisions. Perhaps you and your other heirs will pick one or two people to take the lead. Maybe, you will divide responsibilities so that no one person carries too much of the load. There's no right or wrong answer, just one that makes sense for your family.

In roughly a quarter of the estates I've worked with, mom or dad had set up a trust to dispose of the assets. In that case, the successor trustee (or trustees) has the authority to make decisions about the assets and to sign the necessary documents. For real estate transactions, trusts have advantages over a will because title insurance companies are generally satisfied with the trustee's signature alone.

A quick word on title insurance companies...

They have final authority on many matters.

Almost every home buyer will get title insurance. If they take out a mortgage, they will be required to get lender's title insurance. Title insurance protects the buyer (and lender) from any legal issues regarding previous transfers of the property before the settlement date for the current transaction.

Prior to settlement, the title insurance company will review all legal documents. The title insurance company has the ultimate say on which sellers need to sign in an estate.

If there is a trust, it is quite clear that only the "successor trustees" (the ones named in the trust to take over from your family member) need to sign.

If there is not a will, absent a court order to the contrary, it is almost 100% certain that all heirs will need to sign.

If there is a will, the title company will decide if just the executor can sign or if it will require all the heirs listed in the will to sign the sale paperwork.

Question 2 – Are there any heirs you haven't told me about?

As we've said, if your parent died without a will, state law decides how the assets are divided – usually to a surviving spouse or to surviving children. Under certain circumstances, grandchildren may have the right to share in the assets. So, one of the first things I ask a client is to list ALL of their siblings. And, "all" means "all." That includes any brothers or sisters who have passed away. "All" also includes half-siblings. Perhaps your mom or dad had other marriages or relationships that produced children. Those children may have rights to a share of the estate, and they may need to be involved in decision-making or sign relevant papers regarding a house. "Forgotten" or "unknown" siblings have legal rights and may appear without warning to throw plans into disarray. Leaving aside questions of right or wrong, it's simply bad practice to keep your mouth shut and your fingers crossed.

 Melissa was living with and taking care of her mom in Lorton when her mother passed away without a will. Melissa called me and told me she wanted to remain in the house by paying off the existing mortgage and buying the property. I knew there was no sale here for me, but I could tell she was confused because of a complicated mortgage situation. (More on that later in the book.) I decided to sit with her and offer any real estate guidance I could, but the conversation took a non-mortgage direction very quickly.

When she went to the courthouse to file probate, she was given a sheet which required her to list all heirs. The only name she put down was hers. During our meeting, we were discussing her mom and how Melissa had cared for her mother these last months.

I said something like, "It must have been hard as an only child since you were the only caregiver."

She replied, "Yes it was. I did have a sister, but she passed. I know she would have helped."

I stayed calm, thinking it was not an issue yet. I then asked, "Oh a sister. Did she have any children?"

Melissa said, "Yes, she had 3 sons."

I had to inform Melissa that she had a bigger problem than the mortgage. Her 3 nephews were now co-owners with her and keeping the house wouldn't be as simple as Melissa paying off the mortgage and getting financing in her name. Those 3 boys had to agree to the plan. In this case, Melissa owned only ½ of the house, and each of the boys owned 1/3 of the remaining half. I told her to contact an attorney to verify, but I was pretty sure her plans needed modification.

Now, I truly believe Melissa did not intend to deceive anybody when she didn't list her nephews on the heir form at the courthouse. She honestly assumed that as her mom's only living child all of the assets would go to her.

So, I no longer have casual conversations when there is no will. I come straight out and ask. – "do you have *any* brothers or sisters – living or dead?"

Question 3 –Is the title to the property clear?

One of the big nasty surprises that can pop up in real estate transactions is that the person living in a house they have bought and paid for may not always have a clear title to the house. It's a rare event, but it's a serious problem, and you need to be sure it's not yours. Establishing clear title is why buyers and lenders in real estate transactions require a title search and title insurance.

In a traditional transaction, the contract is signed, the buyer selects a title company, and then the title company runs a title search. When you are selling a house you own, you are familiar with all the details of its purchase and your own financial history, so it is usually safe to wait until you have a contract and have the buyer's title company run a title search. If a problem surfaces, you probably have the paperwork to clear it up.

With an inherited property, however, you may not know the details or the history, so the chances of a surprise are greater. I *always* have a title search run on an inherited property before we put it on the market.

There may be liens or mortgages against the property that the heirs do not know about. It's possible that paid off mortgages were not properly recorded at the courthouse or there could be a recording error in the records. Most of this is immaterial to a person living in a home until.... it is time to sell the home.

If you have a buyer anxious to get into the home and then need to delay settlement to clear title issues, there is a high probability the deal will fall apart. It's very rare that a second contract is better than the first since the initial excitement of the new listing is gone.

The most important advice in this book:

Run a title search before going on the market.

Let me state it again.

Run a title search before going on the market.

Even if you are not going to sell the home but decide to have a family member live there or you decide to keep it as a rental, it would be wise to check the title on an inherited property sooner rather than later. Someday, you or somebody else will want to sell, and the longer title problems fester, the harder they are to solve.

The most common title problem is an "unreleased trust." Let me explain:

House sales typically involve a mortgage. When the mortgage is paid, the paid-in-full note is almost always sent back to the homeowner. However, more often than you would think, the payoff is not recorded at the courthouse. Technically this is called a Certificate of Satisfaction, a one-page document used to release a Deed of Trust (mortgage). It is also sometimes called a Release of Lien.

In the case of an unreleased trust, you will need to come up with documents that demonstrate that the loan was paid. That is easy to do when the house is yours, and you know where you keep important documents. But if you need a payoff letter for a parent's mortgage that was paid off 15 years ago, would you know where to find it? And what if that lender is no longer in business?

Barry inherited a home in Vienna from his godfather, Willie. Willie had purchased the property in 2009 from Hank. Hank had purchased it from George Herman in 1990.

When Hank bought it in 1990, instead of getting a traditional bank loan, he used seller financing. George Herman didn't need all of the money right away, so he agreed to hold the mortgage at a nice interest rate. Effectively, George Herman became the lender, and he received monthly mortgage payments from Hank.

After the 2009 settlement transferring the home from Hank to Willie, it was the responsibility of the title company to pay off the loan balance *and* record the Certificate of Satisfaction at the courthouse. For some reason, the loan was paid off, but it wasn't legally recorded in the courthouse files.

When Barry went to sell the home, he quickly got a contract, but the title search revealed the unreleased trust from the 2009 sale. The current sale could not move forward until it was verified that the earlier loan by George Herman had been paid off. The only way to do that was to find George Herman and have him sign a document stating he had been paid in full.

But no one knew if he was alive or, if he was, where he currently lived.

Barry hired a private detective to track him down, and they found George Herman in a nursing home in Norfolk. He was in very poor health but was of sound mind. He was able to verify the note was paid and the deal closed on time

Now, had they not found George Herman or if he had passed, since Willie had purchased title insurance, the title insurance company would have covered the mistake made by the 2009 settlement company. But initiating that claim and getting it processed would have delayed settlement. And, if Willie did not have title insurance and George Herman wasn't available, Willie could have been on the hook to pay off the loan a second time!!

This happened early in my career before I made probate a niche, but it is one reason that whenever I take on a probate case, I have a title report generated as soon as the listing agreement is signed.

Question 4 – If there are mortgages, what type? (and equity lines count!)

If your parent owed money on the house whether a traditional mortgage, a second mortgage, or a home equity loan, the payments are still due even after his or her death. On some types of loans, like reverse mortgages, the borrower's death may trigger a requirement for an early payoff, so identifying any loan obligations – how much is owed and when it must be paid – should be done as soon as possible. Let me highlight two issues I have seen come up more than once.

REVERSE MORTGAGE LOANS – YOU MUST ACT QUICKLY

Reverse mortgage loans, available only to individuals age 62 or older, enable seniors to stay in their home by giving them access to their equity in the house to meet day-to-day expenses. These loans (formally known as Home Equity Conversion Mortgages or HECMs) can work out very well for seniors, but they can create challenges for their heirs.

In a reverse mortgage, the lender gives money to the borrower, and the home acts as collateral just as in a traditional mortgage. The funds may be disbursed in a lump sum or more typically in monthly payments so that the borrower has a regular income stream. But unlike a regular mortgage, in which monthly mortgage payments reduce the loan principal over time, the principal and interest due on the reverse mortgage go up instead of down. The full balance becomes due upon the death of the borrower or when he/she moves out of the house.

If you inherit a home with a reverse mortgage, you should quickly report the death to the lender and make arrangements for repayment. If you don't report the death, it is very likely the lender will report it to you. They keep track of their home-owners and usually know when someone passes.

The death starts a repayment clock. Frequently that is six months from the date of the death. Sometimes it is less and, under certain circumstances, the due date may be extended for another six months, but that is as far out as the lender is likely to go. Un-like in a traditional mortgage, you cannot simply make monthly payments to keep the loan current until you figure out what to do with the house. With reverse mortgages, the lender is entitled to full payment of the loan in one big chunk. The typical solution for heirs is to sell the house, and they can keep any funds that exceed the amount left on the loan. Given the six-month clock, fast ac-tion is required.

I know every family grieves differently. And I have seen families take months just to go through the personal belongings of their parents. Unfortunately, if there is a reverse mortgage, you don't have the luxury of time. The bank will take the home back when the clock expires.

These loans are typically non-recourse loans, which means the only collateral is the property. If the loan balance is higher than the value of the home, you can just hand the keys to the lender and the estate is not responsible for the shortfall. However, if there is equity, you need to move fast to get the home sold so you can turn that equity into cash. If you dawdle, those dollars that should go into your bank account will disappear.

 Remember Melissa from above – the "only" heir who had a deceased sister with 3 chil-dren. I mentioned that I went to see her be-cause she had a complicated mortgage situ-ation. That complication was a reverse mortgage with an expiring clock.

She was due to receive a very large settlement from an insurance claim that would have allowed her to buy the home free and clear. But getting her hands on the insurance check was taking longer than anticipated. With the added complication of getting her 3 nephews to agree to the sale, she ran out of time and lost the home. There was not a lot of equity there, but for sentimental and practical reasons she wanted to keep the home and could not.

In another instance, Lenny inherited his mother's home, which had well over $50,000 of equity. Her death tore Lenny apart, and he just couldn't get started on the process of attending to her affairs. He ignored the first letter from the mortgage company and then the second. He didn't know she had a reverse mortgage and just figured he would get to the bills and other financial matters when he was mentally prepared.

Then one day he went to the house to find the locks changed. The house had been sold at auction. He called me to see what he could do. I referred him to an attorney. I don't think the lawyer was able to help Lenny because I later saw the house on the market after being remodeled by the investor who had purchased it at auction.

SECOND MORTGAGES AND EQUITY LOANS COUNT

I have had more than one heir tell me that there was only one mortgage when more than one existed. It wasn't that they were trying to be deceitful, they just didn't know

Jason inherited a home worth $500,000 with what he thought was $200,000 in equity. The title search we ran before going on the market found a home equity loan with a $200,000 balance –effectively wiping out all of the equity Jason thought would wind up in his pocket. "That matters?" Jason asked me. I sadly informed him that it did because debts don't go away with death. Since he wasn't going to net out any gain, he decided it wasn't worth the time and energy to put the house up for sale, so he turned over the keys to the bank.

Another client, Sharon was able to sell her property despite being surprised to learn 2nd trusts matter. She inherited a home with what she thought was $225,000 in equity. In this case, the 2nd trust was only $50,000, much less than the equity in the house, so she still wound up with a pretty nice inheritance of $175,000. When I asked Sharon why she hadn't told me about it, she mentioned that that bank told her she wasn't responsible for it.

Sharon, not a homeowner, knew that a "mortgage" is tied to a home. But she wondered if the bills she saw for an "equity line" also needed to be paid. She called the bank, and I assume that the conversation with the bank went something like this.

Sharon, "Am I responsible for the equity line."

The bank employee answered, "No you are not" thinking that Sharon was asking if she was *personally* responsible for the equity line. I imagine the bank employee thought *everyone* knew that equity lines were the same as mortgages. Sharon was not personally responsible for the equity line, but the estate surely was. Sharon innocently misunderstood the situation.

So when I asked how many mortgages, Sharon, of course, said just one.

Ideally, you won't have any surprises like these, but when a Realtor ® or other adviser asks you questions about finances, he or she isn't being nosy or insensitive, they're trying to prevent problems.

Question 5 – Does the deceased or any of the heirs have outstanding judgments against them?

In every real estate transaction, a title abstractor, the person who goes to the court and checks on the title, not only researches the house but researches the owners as well. This is because judgments against the owner can be attached to the house. A seller cannot sell until any outstanding judgments are satisfied. If judgments surface, typically at settlement, the judgment amount is subtracted from the seller's proceeds.

Clearing judgments are part of delivering a clear title to a buyer, who must be confident that a debt owed by the prior owner will not adversely affect his ownership of the home.

This is another reason to run a title search. Was the family member who left you the house involved in some kind of lawsuit they never told you about? Has a creditor secured a judgment for an outstanding debt? Some of these issues may have been embarrassing and not been discussed within the family. Better to find this out at the beginning of the process than after a contract has been accepted.

In an estate, the search doesn't stop with the person who passed away. The abstractor will search for judgments against heirs as well.

Why? Upon death, the house immediately becomes the property of the heirs. They may not be able to sell it until probate starts, or other matters are cleared up, but some person or a legal entity such as a trust needs to be the official "homeowner." Upon the death of the prior homeowner, the heirs automatically become the new owners. As "owners" of the home, a judgment against an heir must be satisfied just like a judgment against the deceased.

Important note: Judgments against heirs are not relevant if the home was owned in a trust since the trust is still "alive" after the death of the parent who had set up the trust. There was no transfer of ownership at the time of the death of your parent – only the name of the trustee changed. To the world, and in the courthouse records, ownership remains in the trust. The details of a trust are not in the public record like a will so abstractors and others would have no idea of the name of the successor trustee.

Vince, Joe, and Dom inherited their father's home in Annandale in 2017. It was owned free and clear and valued at $600,000. Vince had an outstanding court judgment against him for $2,000 dating back to 1999 involving a disputed auto repair. Over time, interest for the non-payment had increased the amount due to $6,000. We could not sell unless Vince agreed to pay the judgment. Vince was divorced and said that it was his ex-wife's fault and that she told him the debt had been paid. I said: "I don't care why it happened or who should have done what. You have to pay it, get her to pay it, negotiate a settlement or have your brothers pay it but we can't sell the house until you do. Somehow the judgment needs to be cleared." He begrudgingly agreed to have it come out of his share, and we moved forward.

That size of the judgment here was small and not a show stopper. But the experience reinforced my belief in getting get all the facts on the table as soon as possible.

Good information leads to better decisions. Surprises can force you into inferior options.

Question 6. Do all heirs agree on what to do or are they at least agreeable about discussing options?

Now that you have most of the facts regarding the circumstances, it's time to decide what to do – hold, rent, or sell. Making this decision depends on both financial and personal circumstances. In my experience, most heirs wind up selling the property. But that doesn't necessarily mean selling is the right choice for you. My job is to help you through the thought process. And, that process begins with one fundamental reality. Remember, in most cases, *all* heirs must agree.

Joe Facenda

When there is more than one heir whether, by a will or most certainly when there is no will, it's likely that the house is left jointly to the survivors. Typically, each has a share in that property, and that means each has a say in what to do with it. Unlike liquid assets such as stocks and bonds that are easily divided so that each heir has exclusive control of their share, houses can't be divvied up. That means each heir has veto power. Heirs can vote eight to one to sell the house, but unless the dissenter agrees to go along and sign the necessary documents, nothing happens. The heirs could go to court and seek a "partition action" to allow the eight to have their way. But this would be expensive, emotionally taxing, and time-consuming for all involved. Plus, they might not win.

Most families find ways to work it out, but it can get messy and emotional, especially if it's the house you grew up in. Some family members may be reluctant to sell because of the good memories associated with it. Others may feel they deserve a larger share or bigger say because they were "closer" to mom or dad or became the primary caregiver in their final years. Old animosities or emotional wounds may also get in the way.

If your parents had children from other relationship, that could complicate matters as well.

 Lisa, Erica and Monique's father passed without a will. He had been divorced from their mother for 23 years and was unmarried when he died. So, the three sisters inherited the home. The sisters all lived in different states than their dad. I met with two of the three when they came to Virginia to clean out the home.

They agreed to work with me, and I went through all of my usual questions including "Are there any other heirs." The two sisters looked funny at each other and responded, "None that we know of." I was a little uncomfortable with the answer and related the story about Melissa - the women with the dead sister and 3 nephews. They said, "Not our family."

As usual, before going on the market, we ran a title report.

Surprise, surprise. After the divorce, their Dad had a girlfriend, and the two of them had a son. That son, Anthony, was due ¼ of the estate. Thinking that his sisters who had not had a relationship with him would try to squeeze him out, he hired an attorney to ensure he got his share of the estate. The title abstractor found the filing in the courthouse records.

For years, Erica had been angry with her dad for leaving her mom, and there was "no way" she was going to share her inheritance with "illegitimate" Anthony. For a time, she refused to sign documents agreeing to a four-way split of the proceeds. She didn't want the half-brother involved at all. Eventually, she came around, but there were some tough moments getting there.

The point of the above story is that all heirs must agree. It is not unusual in a family that siblings have different goals or those old rivalries or long suppressed anger surfaces. But heirs have to find a way to push aside their grievances and agree on a course of action because the house can't be sold until they do.

Differing financial situations or money habits also can add complications. I've worked with families where one family member, perhaps well off, wanted to move as fast as possible even if it meant a smaller financial return while others needed to get every penny possible. As a Realtor, I cannot decide which approach is better, because all of the siblings are equally my clients. My job is to point out the consequences of various decisions in the hope that the information will help the family members settle on a course of action.

PART 2: KEEP IT, RENT IT OR SELL IT.

Those are the three basic choices. As previously mentioned, there is sometimes a 4th which is to hand it over to the bank. If you are thinking about letting the bank take the property you MUST talk with an estate attorney and a tax professional to make sure you aren't triggering any unintended consequences that will cost you money or lead to other regrets.

Sticking with the three main options, let's analyze each.

SHOULD YOU KEEP THE HOUSE?

It might be that one of the heirs was living in the house with mom or dad when your parent passed away. Or, somebody in the family thinks moving into the vacant house would make sense. This can be a good outcome that avoids the work associated with getting a house ready to sell. But like every other option, it requires agreement among the heirs.

The family may readily agree that one (or more) of the heirs can live in the house, but that requires agreement on whether the other heirs should be compensated and how to arrange it. That might mean that one heir buys out the others. The heirs might agree to some alternative arrangement that lets the heir who is keeping the house pay for it over time. Or, the heir who wants the house might take out a mortgage.

Whatever the arrangement, it's best to treat it like any other real estate transaction by arranging for a title search and drawing up the same documentation and loan agreements as if you are dealing with a stranger. If you're too loose about these things or say "we can all trust each other" you will open the door to misunderstanding or disagreements down the road. Even without malice, memories can fade, or people sometimes understand informal agreements differently.

And please get an official appraisal. For tax reasons, it is extremely important to establish the value of the home at the time of death. A Realtor can provide an opinion of value, but if you are not selling, the better way to go is to get an appraisal from a licensed appraiser.

If the family member buys the house above or below the appraisal, there may be tax implications. For this option, it's a good idea to have a tax advisor on your team.

> *Should I get an appraisal?*   If you are selling, there are differing opinions as to whether or not you need an appraisal. I know for certain that determining the value at the time of death is important. However, different tax advisers have different opinions on how to document that number. Many will say that if you sell on the open market shortly after death, the market has determined the value. Others will still want an appraisal. Consult your adviser to help figure out your best course of action.

SHOULD YOU BECOME A LAND-
LORD AND RENT THE HOUSE?

Turning the house into a rental property may be a reasonable option if the house is fully paid off or if the monthly rent would cover the monthly mortgage payments. The heirs may like the idea of receiving a rent check every month while also retaining the chance to benefit from a continued appreciation of the property.

I'm a big fan of rental property as an investment strategy. In fact, my personal retirement planning includes a few modest rental properties that I hope will provide me with regular income once I stop working.

But renting an inherited property vs. deliberately searching for and selecting an investment property is not the same. In my opinion, you should evaluate the inherited property's rental potential as if it hadn't belonged to a member of the family.

Is the house in good enough shape to make a good rental or will it require expensive upgrades and repairs before you can hang a "For Rent" sign?

If this home were on the open market, would you buy it as an investment?

Aside from the numbers, there may be emotional considerations in renting out your parent's home that you don't have in with a traditional rental property. You have to be prepared for the likelihood that the tenant won't treat the house with the same care as your family did. Will that bother you?

You need to know your goals. Is this a long term hold or a short term investment until other issues are worked out?

Preparing a house for sale vs. renting involves different strategies. Getting a home rent ready focuses more on making sure everything works, and it is relatively attractive. Getting it ready for sale often means a bigger investment for cosmetic repairs and/or upgrades that might not fare well in a tenant-occupied house. Things like a higher quality flooring or upgraded cabinets and appliances may not make sense for a rental but could be a requirement for sale.

Also to be considered is the fact that unless you're the sole heir, turning your parent's house into a rental property means you will be going into business with other heirs. If you all approach money decisions the same way, have the same tolerance for spending on upkeep and repairs, and have similar goals, congratulations because you may have the makings of a great partnership.

It's also possible that you and your relatives won't mesh as business partners. One relative might prefer to do minimal repairs, keep costs low and collect lower rents. Another may want to invest more up-front to attract higher rents from a more affluent clientele.

One more thing: while all may agree *today* that renting mom's house is a great idea, financial situations and investment strategies can change. One sibling may grow tired of the rental business. Another may face unexpected expenses and need to get cash out of the house. Real estate is not liquid. If one member of the family suddenly wants out, the other family members may have to come up with money to buy her out or be forced to sell when they don't want to.

Entering a business partnership based primarily on sharing ancestry doesn't always work out well.

Recently, Mark, his younger brother Sam, and Mark's son, Jacob asked me for help with a home they'd inherited. The brothers liked the idea of renting because of emotional attachment to the house they'd grown up in. But Jacob, who was business savvy, told me privately that his uncle had trouble managing his personal finances, was struggling with debt, and often needed money from relatives just to make ends meet. To me, those were yellow caution lights flashing "Watch Out."

I tried to persuade them to sell the home but two of the three wanted to keep it, and so I never put it on the market. I hope that the good relations between the family members remain intact and that Sam, the next time he needs money, does not suddenly insist on getting cash for his third of the home.

I mentioned above that it may be wise to look at the home

strictly by the numbers. Yes, there is an emotional component and if the numbers are borderline perhaps that tips the scales in favor of keeping the property. But, please, please, please, get the numbers straight before you make a decision.

Also, I suggest you consider that if you have inherited a $500,000 home, you didn't really inherit a $500,000 home. You inherited $500,000 that just happens to be tied up in a house – and you have the option to turn that asset into cash. If you don't need that money for other purposes and want to invest it ask yourself if this home is the best use of those funds?

 Betsy inherited a $500,000 home from her mother and was seriously thinking of keeping it as a rental. True she had some emotional attachment to the home, but she also thought it was in a good area and would appreciate nicely over the next few years. I respected her feelings but suggested we put aside the emotional part. I asked her to look at the numbers.

I don't want to get into a detailed discussion on analyzing rental returns, but briefly: she had a $500,000 asset that was free and clear. She could keep it and get about $2,700 a month in rent... OR.... She could sell it, stay local and buy two $250,000 properties and rent each for $1,500 to $1,600..... OR... she could invest in other markets around the country and buy four $125,000 properties that rent for $1000 each. She also had the option of other types of investments such as stocks or something very safe like U.S. Treasury bonds.

Additionally, I pointed out that when you have one property, and it is vacant, your vacancy rate is 100% and income $0. With multiple properties, 1 vacancy reduces your cash flow but doesn't eliminate it.

She eventually understood and decided to sell.

Yes, I know there are transactional costs and out-of-town rentals probably mean you will need to hire a property manager. But the bottom line is that if you think of the $500,000 as cash available for investment it might be underutilized if it is all kept in the family home.

Last, going into the rental business will have tax implications. The rent is income, and Uncle Sam will want his share every year. Perhaps more importantly, and sometimes overlooked in the decision process, is the possibility of significant capital gains taxes down the road.

When a family member dies and leaves a house as part of his or her estate, the heirs inherit the home at a "stepped up basis." This means that you get it at market value as of the date of your family member's passing. If you sell within a reasonable time of the death, there is no taxable gain, and the heirs can keep the proceeds without paying taxes. If you hang onto the house and it increases in value (as you hope), and you sell it, later on, that gain is taxable. While making a financial decision *solely* on taxes is rarely the right way to decide on an investment, it should be part of the equation.

(This is a simplified discussion of stepped-up basis. Please consult a tax professional to review your specific situation.)

Bottom line: Being a landlord is a business. Before you sign on the dotted line, ask yourself – do you want to be in this business, does it fit with your long-term financial goals, and are you reasonably confident that your siblings and any other co-heirs – all of them – would be good business partners?

SHOULD YOU SELL?

Most people sell. More often than not, people who inherit a home already have a place to live and aren't looking to move. Quite frequently, one or more of the heirs live in a different state than mom or dad and holding onto the house just creates a distant asset they have to worry about.

When deciding to sell an inherited home, there are likely to be a few more decisions to make than with a traditional home. After going through the legal legwork mentioned above and consulting with family members about the right course of action, the next step is to assess the home and decide which market you should appeal to – investor or owner-occupant.

Every house will sell if the price matches the condition. In order to do that, you have to try to look through a buyer's eyes to see what kind of house you are offering. Is the home obsolete, a show-case, or somewhere in between?

This assessment requires a minimum of emotion. Placing a house in one of these categories isn't a value judgment about your parent, your sibling, or you. Your family member may have taken tremendous care of the home for years but as their health started to decline or their finances got tighter, maintenance items were left undone, and the garden out front became overgrown. Perhaps they preferred to spend their money on things other than their house. Being honest about the condition is not a statement on your family but a reality that needs to be faced.

Selling a house should be an exercise in realism.

So, let's talk about the three categories and what each one means for your sales strategy.

The Obsolete Home

An "obsolete home" may be structurally sound, but it has elements that make it relatively unattractive for somebody looking for a place to move into immediately. In fact, it may not be livable in its current condition.

It may have been a great place to grow up in its prime, and it may have met your parent's needs even though it lacked some modern conveniences. But a new buyer may have different expectations than somebody who has lived in a house for many years and was used to the outdated layout or quirky mechanics.

An obsolete house has a solid foundation and should still be standing decades in the future, but it is old and faded. Its basic infrastructure – kitchen, bathroom, appliances, heating, and cooling system – is largely outdated and the house will need a lot of work, beyond the cosmetic, to bring it up to today's standards. It's not just that the paint is dingy or the wallpaper faded, but that major systems need updating and/or repairs.

Often, elderly owners lack the money or the interest to take care of these items. They've been living with the same stove for 20 years, and as long as it works, they're content. They don't see any reason for a double-vanity in their bathroom. Why have central air when window units are just fine? Small closets came with the house, and it worked for the family. Perhaps in their later years, mom and dad simply didn't want to put any money into the home. They might have been living on a limited fixed budget, or maybe, they preferred to spend money on the grandkids or nice vacations instead of the house.

It really doesn't matter why the house is in a particular condition. Your challenge now is to make the right decision, and that begins by honestly assessing the house for what it is and isn't.

Often is it not worth putting any money into a home like this. Unless you plan to execute a full renovation, it is best to just clean it out and do a little spruce up to boost the curb appeal. Leave the rest of it to the buyer after he or she moves in. Painting one room or replacing the carpet in another will be a waste of money if the kitchen and baths are outdated.

I've worked with heirs who wanted to do major remodels so they could sell for top dollar. But unless you or someone in the family is licensed contractor and/or has remodeling experience, the extra money you might earn will almost always be less than you think. We've all seen the TV shows about folks making a bundle by sprucing up rundown homes, but it's not as simple or as certain as it appears on television.

There are non-financial considerations to take into account as well.

After factoring in your time, stress, and potential fights with siblings over details such as cabinet choices and carpeting, it might end up being wiser to sell as is. Plus if there are multiple heirs, how much is each extra dollar worth to each heir?

Many sellers think they can't sell a rundown home easily. To be honest, a rundown house is one of the easier homes to sell if priced right. There are dozens of investors in the market who look for just these types of homes, and the supply is often limited. (More about investors a bit later.) Plus, there are also many do-it-yourself owner-occupants who would jump at a chance to buy at a discount and, over time, benefit from sweat equity.

The owner-occupant will always pay a little more than the investor because the transactional costs are less and they don't have to do everything all at once. Perhaps the owner-occupant will fix up the kitchen and upper-level baths immediately but wait a year or two before tackling the basement. An investor, to flip a home, needs to make everything perfect all at once.

When I price a home like this, I look at what it would bring if everything was updated entirely and come up with the after-repair value or ARV. Then I ballpark the repair costs and subtract those from the ARV. After that, I deduct an additional amount for the sweat equity that an owner-occupant would hope to get as a return for her work. That would be our list price.

For an investor, we replace the words "sweat equity" with the word "profit." The process starts the same as for an owner-occupant, but we don't stop there. There are additional numbers to subtract from the ARV when pricing for an investor. We need to factor in her acquisition costs, the cost of money (borrowing costs/interest) and the cost involved in selling the house after remodel. So the price you can get an investor to pay is almost certainly much lower than the number for selling to an owner-occupant.

That said, I have experienced cases where I priced for an owner-occupant, and an investor bought the home. Each investor has her own cost of money and labor charges. And each has a different number in mind for an acceptable profit. Try as I might, there is variability in determining the right price for an investor sale. The "right" number is not the same for every investor.

Many of these obsolete homes can sell to either an investor or an owner-occupant, but some are so run down that they need to be priced specifically for investors. An experienced Realtor can help you determine which category your house falls into.

Also, a Realtor will be able to tell you if you should avoid certain types of financing. Federal Housing Administration (FHA) and Veterans Administration (VA) loans are attractive to buyers because they offer zero down payment or low down payment options and often have lower interest rates. But these loans require most items in the house to be in working order.

That means accepting FHA or VA financing for homes in rough condition will generate problems for the seller when the appraiser reports the condition to the lender. The lender, as a condition of the loan, will require certain items to be repaired which will negate the benefits of selling as is. If you have non-working heating, no hot water, a leaking roof, rotted trim or a host of other issues a VA or FHA loan is not a viable option. The only way to get to settlement with those types of loans is to correct all the issues – and that costs money. I have seen situations where buyers will pay for these repairs, but that opens a whole different set of problems like who selects the contractors and what if settlement doesn't happen or what if someone is hurt on the job. It's best to stay away from these loans for homes needing significant work.

One last thought on obsolete detached homes. In many neighborhoods in Northern Virginia, the land is worth more than the home. If you see teardowns in the neighborhood, make sure you look at the numbers both ways. What could you get for the lot and what would you get for the home? Sometimes the home is worth more dead and torn down than alive. In that case, it's not worth it to put money into the house. What you want is a buyer or builder who is looking for a place to build a new house.

Everywhere you turn where I live in Vienna, houses are being torn down. Homes for $1.5 million and more are being built on quarter acre lots all over town. This means that the lot itself is worth about $600,000.

I got a call from an executor who had an obsolete home on one of these lots. I knew the floor plan of the existing home and knew that in perfect condition it would sell for close to $700,000. I asked if I could get into the house to assess the cost of repairs. He told me there was no need and suggested I walk around the outside and know that the inside was much worse. Well, just looking at the outside and doing a quick guess about the inside, I knew we were well past $100,000 in repairs, so it was an easy decision – forget about spending on repairs and sell it to a builder who would immediately tear it down.

An additional advantage when selling to a builder whose only interest is the land is that you don't need to clean out the house. If it is in horrible shape and is a complete gut job or a teardown, the first thing the buyer will do is drop off a dumpster. They can throw away old clothes, broken furniture, and moldy rugs along with the torn down cabinets and old appliances. But make sure you look everywhere for valuables......

Beth's dad was a great gardener and very handy around the home until illness took away most of his physical abilities. Stuff just started to pile up in the home when he lost the ability to tidy up. Beth lived far away, and her dad refused her suggestions to arrange for a caregiver. When he passed, the home was in disrepair, and some might have said it resembled a hoarder home. The only realistic choice was selling to an investor. We priced it accordingly, and it sold quickly. Beth was also very happy she didn't have to pay for the junk to be removed. The contractor said they would dispose of everything as they were stripping it to the studs. Before settlement, Beth drove to the house, found the items of value and personal meaning, loaded them on her truck and headed back to Vermont. Then a few weeks after settlement I got a call from the new owner asking me where he should send the $5000 in bonds he found in the office desk.....

The Showcase

On the opposite end of the spectrum is the completely updated model home. This is easy. If your parent left you a well-maintained and upgraded house with a kitchen and bathrooms that meet today's standards you should be able to sell with relative speed and ease. Yes, there are likely to be some fixes required here and there. The house may need some fresh paint; an appliance or two may need replacing. Your Realtor can help you decide which investments will pay off with either a quicker sale or a higher price. Overall, if you have inherited a showcase and the house has cleared the title search, the biggest challenge left is figuring out the right price.

Depending on the number of heirs, market conditions and how quickly you want to sell, you might even list it at the lower end of the possible price range. Consider this: the more heirs involved, the smaller the value of a higher price. Another $10,000 is a nice added chunk of change for a single heir or even when split two ways, but if you have five heirs splitting the pot, you may prefer moving the property more quickly vs. letting it sit for an extra $2,000 per heir. The answer to that question will naturally vary depending on the individuals involved and the amount of extra money at stake. But, it's a consideration to take account of.

In estate sales with multiple heirs, there are often conflicting goals. One heir may want it done as fast as possible and is willing to sacrifice some profit to wrap things up, but a different heir may be in a financial jam and need every dollar. No right or wrong answer and no judgment, just a frequent reality of pricing with multiple heirs.

As a side note, it is counter-intuitive but depending upon the market, when a home is priced at the lower end of the acceptable range, it may attract more attention, gather multiple offers, and end up selling for more than it would have if priced higher. This is especially important to think about when the inventory of available homes is low. Appropriate pricing strategy for the current market is another element your Realtor can help you with.

The In-Between House

This is the toughest house to figure out and sell. The in-between house is in good enough shape that a buyer can imagine moving in with some adjustments. You likely will not be offering this home at a substantial discount so it won't appeal to the sweat equity buyers. And it probably doesn't make financial sense to do extensive updating to try to compete with a showcase house.

This home is one that perhaps has an updated kitchen and master bath, but the hall bath is dated. Or the main level has great hardwood floors and is freshly painted while the basement has cheap paneling and 1980s carpet. It is almost there, but not quite.

Maybe it is best to go beyond cosmetic repairs to drive up the price a bit. The challenge is to find the line between doing enough and stopping before spending more than you will get back in return. It's an inexact science, but your Realtor can guide you along.

Some things are easy and relatively inexpensive to fix – you can steam off old wallpaper, apply fresh paint and install some new carpeting without huge expense. You may want to add some curb appeal so that perspective buyers will get out of the car. Putting down a layer of fresh mulch in the flower beds and planting new flowers if it's the right time of year can go a long way at modest expense.

But deciding whether to remodel that other bath or drywall the basement or get a new HVAC are tougher calls. Up to a point, the more you put in, the more you get back. Upgrading kitchens and bathrooms can be costly, but there's a good chance you will recover those dollars with a higher sales price. New windows with double or triple insulation are a great investment for a homeowner, but they rarely add enough to the sales price to be worth it to the seller.

There is a market for houses in this category. Since this home will not be priced at the top of the market, there is a chance that price-sensitive buyers who are attracted to the neighborhood but can't afford a showcase will be excited about the in-between home.

The "right" answers won't be the same in every neighborhood. If the house is in a costly or popular neighborhood, buyers will expect more for their money. If the house is in a more modest neighborhood, you have to be careful not to put in so many amenities that the house is out of sync with those around it. Generally, buyers will not pay top dollar to be surrounded by neighboring homes that are worth much less.

Deciding how much to invest in upgrades and repairs requires you to assess the neighborhood, look at the sales prices of comparable homes, consider how much money you and any other heirs have available for repairs, and then make a judgment call. A Realtor who knows the neighborhood can help you figure it out.

SELLING TO AN INVESTOR –
TREAD CAREFULLY

How much you want to invest in fixing up your inherited house is partly about priorities. Is it more important to you to sell fast or to get top dollar? Perhaps you simply don't have the money to spend on improving the house. If you need to sell fast (remember the reverse mortgage discussion earlier) or don't have the money, you may want to target the investor market even though the sale

37

price will almost certainly be lower. Or there may be very unique circumstances that dictate a quick sale. Investors almost always settle faster than owner-occupants.

Jackson inherited two homes. His dad had lived in a small townhome in Herndon and also owned a large single family home in Centreville that he rented out. After reviewing his dad's papers, he realized he needed to raise cash fast to save the Centreville home.

The Herndon townhome was is rough shape. Parts were completely remodeled, but others were completely torn up because as Jackson's dad, who was doing the remodel himself, had taken ill and was never able to complete the job. Although the townhome was owned free and clear of any mortgage payments, there was very little cash in the estate so completing the remodel work was not financially possible.

The rental home was a different story. The tenants knew of their landlord's illness and thought that made it safe to stop paying rent.

The tenants were several months behind. Without the rental income and faced with mounting medical bills, Jackson's father hadn't had money to make mortgage payments in his last months. Nor, did he have the energy to pursue the tenants. As a result, the Centreville house was close to foreclosure

The solution – sell the Herndon townhouse to an investor to unlock the cash in a property that was owned free and clear; use the proceeds to bring the Centreville mortgage up to date, evict the tenants, spruce up the home and sell at a profit. And that is what we did.

Even if the condition of the house is so bad or the situation dictates that the investor market is your only realistic choice, you will almost always do better if you make investors compete for your property. A Realtor who is familiar with the local investment community can usually drive up the price by getting multiple bids. Investors have different strategies and an agent who knows the investing community should be able to get you a better deal.

As an executor or administrator, your contact information is in the public record. I am sure you will receive several pieces of mail or phone calls from investors with "we pay cash" offers. At first blush, these blind offers may seem like an appealing way to sell a house fast. You can easily accept those without involving a Realtor. However, almost always, putting the home on the open market will get you a better return and you can sell just as quickly. Reaching out to a range of investors, even after paying a Realtor, should net you more than taking the first "we pay cash" offer.

When targeting investors, please remember.

An investor needs to buy at the lowest price possible.

A Realtor wants to get you the highest price possible.

MIGHT YOU LET THE BANK
HAVE THE HOUSE?

There is one final option when you inherit a home. Sometimes, mortgage loans may exceed the value of the home. In that case, the smartest financial decision may be to sign the deed over to the bank.

If your parent or other family member lived in the house for a long time and financed it with a mortgage, chances are there is enough equity to make a sale viable. But if he or she took out multiple mortgages or wasn't in the house long enough to build much equity, the situation may be more complex. If he bought at the high point in the housing market and the value of the house has declined – as happened to many Americans during the 2008 financial crisis – the home may be "underwater" and walking away may then become a logical decision.

Before deciding to just hand over the keys, you **must** talk to an estate attorney and a tax advisor. Also, as an executor, you have a responsibility to the estate and want to make sure you are not missing anything or harming the other heirs by giving the house to the bank.

I have seen a few cases where families have given an underwater house back to the bank, and I have seen situations where a home with little or no equity was sold. That decision needs to be made with the guidance of other professionals.

DO YOU NEED PROFESSIONAL ASSISTANCE?

Can you do this on your own or should you engage professional assistance? I am a Realtor, so you can probably guess what I think.

Leaving my professional bias aside, there are several reasons I think the answer is almost always "yes." However, there is the occasional situation where I think an heir can do just fine proceeding on his own. Typically, those situations involve run down, obsolete homes that will be sold to an investor.

I have occasionally met with an heir who has an offer in hand from an investor. As I said before, usually you will get more on the open market even when targeting an investor. I also noted that each investor has his or her own profit margin and labor costs. However, once in a while, the cash offer is so good I know it can't be beaten on the street. In those situations, I graciously step away.

With today's modern communications tools, it's easy to find online tutorials and a range of do-it-yourself guides for almost any type of transaction, including selling a house. Since that avoids Realtor commission, some folks are tempted to try it.

But a Realtor experienced with probate can make the process easier and more financially rewarding than if you do it yourself. If you've sold a house on your own before, live near the inherited property, are the only heir, and know the local marketplace doing it yourself might work out. But, as I've discussed throughout this book, there are many minefields with inherited real estate.

Even traditional transactions have become more complicated over the years because of required disclosures and documentation that a do-it-yourself seller may not know about. Not knowing all the rules can create legal liability even when you do the best you can. Add in the twists and turns of probate plus all of the other tasks one has to complete when closing out an estate, hiring a real estate professional to help you with an inherited house should reduce stress, protect you from mistakes and usually nets you a better return.

Furthermore, if there are multiple heirs and you are the executor you owe it to the other heirs to ensure you are getting the best result for all involved. The only way to do that is to put it on the market or in some other way expose it to multiple buyers.

Last story....

Uncle Henry was named in the will as executor for his brother's estate. His brother had two children who lived out of state, and Henry lived near his brother's home in Alexandria. All proceeds were going to his nephews. Henry wouldn't get any personal financial benefit from the work involved in selling the house. His only compensation for putting would be the fee he received as executor.

The home was slightly rundown. It wasn't quite obsolete, but it was very close to the line. Henry thought it was worse than it was. Either his standards were high, or he had overestimated what it would take to get it in great shape.

In any event, he only wanted to sell to investors. An investor I know contacted Henry in his normal course of business and arranged to see the house. He made Henry an offer that made sense for the investor but was much less than what the house could have sold for on the open market.

With about $75,000 in work, the house could have sold for about $900,000. But Uncle Henry settled for $690,000. If Uncle Henry had engaged a Realtor, I am confident he could have put the house on the market for somewhere between $775,000 and $800,000 – without upgrades – and sold to an owner-occupant looking to get into the neighborhood at a discount.

But it seemed his priority was to wrap up the estate as quickly as possible and the low-ball investor offer accomplished that. Maybe there was a part of the story I didn't know about. Perhaps everyone was happy in the end but what if a family member found out that Uncle Henry had left money on the table? Hiring a Realtor tends to disprove any subsequent claim that you, as the executor, took a shortcut instead of getting the best deal for the estate.

So, how do you select a Realtor?

For traditional sales, perhaps the best method is getting a referral from a friend or neighbor. But in the probate world, you will be better served by somebody who knows the quirks involved in handling inherited property.

Here's my advice:

First, consider how long a prospective agent has have been licensed. If less than three years, I would pass. In my opinion, the first few years are learning years for a Realtor. Some wonderful Realtors get off to a fast start and provide outstanding service. However, probate is complicated. I can't imagine a relative newcomer has seen enough of the minefields in a traditional transaction, let alone the issues that come with estate sales.

Observe the Realtor when they walk your property particularly if the house needs work. I know of colleagues who believe every home needs to be a showcase. If your house isn't in that category and the Realtor is recommending a lot of costly improvements, you should take a step back and think hard. Ugly houses scare some listing agents into suggesting too many changes because they are afraid that it will take too much work on their part to sell. But the truth is, if priced right, there is a strong market for these homes.

Assuming they have been licensed for several years and are not scared by the house you are offering, ask about their probate experience.

Here are three questions that will tell you if they know what they are talking about.

Q. Are there any extra settlement charges for selling a home while in probate?

A. If you have a will or the deceased died without a will, the answer is "yes" if the death occurred within one year of the planned settlement date on your sale. In order to collect the sale proceeds at settlement, the title insurance company for the buyer will require the estate to pay a bond of $2 per thousand of the sale price. On a $500,000 house that works out to $1,000 that effectively comes right out of the heirs' pocket.

If the estate doesn't need the money immediately or you are close to the first anniversary, you can decide to not pay the bond, and the title company will hold the proceeds until you reach the one year mark. I have had cases where the settlement was within a month of the 1st anniversary, and the heirs were not in immediate need of the proceeds, so they left the money in escrow to avoid the extra charge.

The choice to take the proceeds immediately or keep it in escrow is up to the heirs. And like every other decision, all must agree. It is isn't that one heir takes the money now and the others can wait.

If the home is in a trust, the answer is - no extra charge.

Q. Can the title company send the proceeds to any account you choose or do you need to set up an estate account?

A. It depends.

The title companies make the rules on these things. One of their jobs is to collect all of the money and then send it where it legally needs to go. I have dealt with title companies that will only issue checks in the name of the seller which is often "Estate of..." Others are comfortable sending the money to other accounts providing they are given proper written instructions.

In Virginia, the buyer gets to select the title company so, if you want the proceeds sent to multiple accounts, it's helpful to know the title company's policy before accepting a contract.

Q. I've sold homes before and understand what's involved in a traditional house sale. Is there anything different we should do with an inherited house before going on the market?

A. If they do not answer "run a title report," then you should run. Any agent with more than a handful of probate transactions knows that the things that you don't know about can derail this type of sale. Like I said, the most important point in this book was to avoid untimely surprises by running a title report before going on the market.

If they answer those three questions correctly, have years of experience as a Realtor and supply references of probate homes they have worked on, you should be in good shape.

LAST THOUGHTS

I hope you have found this book helpful. We covered several different situations, but I know that every situation is unique in its own way, and requires us, together, to come up with creative solutions. That individuality is what I love about helping people with inherited property.

If you have a situation not covered in this book, feel free to reach out to me for guidance or with any questions.

Of course, if the home is in Northern Virginia, I am happy to meet with you and if selling is the right option, to represent you in the transaction.

If selling is not the right option or you just need to talk, I am happy to do what I can to assist.

Once you have signed with another Realtor, ethically, I can't offer advice. However, even if you know you will not be using me as your Realtor and want some advice before you talk to your Realtor of choice, feel free to get in touch.

These are difficult and sensitive times, and I want to be a resource whether or not it will result in a professional relationship.

Feel free to contact me anytime at Joe@JoeFacenda.com

Made in the USA
Middletown, DE
23 June 2019